T0088405

Gabriel Jackson

THE WORLD IMAGINED

MUSIC DEPARTMENT

OXFORD
UNIVERSITY PRESS

OXFORD
UNIVERSITY PRESS

Great Clarendon Street, Oxford OX2 6DP,
United Kingdom

Oxford University Press is a department of the University of Oxford.
It furthers the University's objective of excellence in research, scholarship,
and education by publishing worldwide. Oxford is a registered trade mark of
Oxford University Press in the UK and in certain other countries

© Oxford University Press 2021

Gabriel Jackson has asserted his right under the Copyright,
Designs and Patents Act, 1988, to be identified as the Composer of this Work

First published 2021

Impression: 1

All rights reserved. No part of this publication may be reproduced,
stored in a retrieval system, or transmitted, in any form or by any means,
without the prior permission in writing of Oxford University Press

Permission to perform this work in public (except in the course of divine worship)
should normally be obtained from a local performing right licensing organization,
unless the owner or the occupier of the premises being used already holds a licence
from such an organization. Likewise, permission to make and exploit a recording of this work
should be obtained from a local mechanical copyright licensing organization

Enquiries concerning reproduction outside the scope of the above
should be directed to the Music Rights Department, Oxford University Press,
at music.permissions.uk@oup.com or at the address above

ISBN 978-0-19-354020-0

Music and text origination by Andrew Jones

Printed in Great Britain on acid-free paper by
Halstan & Co. Ltd, Amersham, Bucks.

Contents

Duration: *c.*43 minutes

Instrumentation

Piccolo
2 Flutes
2 Oboes
Cor Anglais
2 Clarinets in B♭
Bass Clarinet
2 Bassoons
Contrabassoon

4 Horns in F
3 Trumpets in C
2 Tenor Trombones
Bass Trombone
Tuba

3 Percussion:
1.   Tam-tam
       Vibraphone
       Suspended Cymbal
       Triangle
       3 Woodblocks
       Vibraslap
2.   Crotales
       Bass Drum
       Mark Tree
       Sandpaper Blocks
       Claves
3.   Tubular Bells
       Glockenspiel
       Chinese Cymbal (with Double Bass bow)
       Brake Drum
       Whip

Harp

Strings

Full scores, vocal scores, and instrumental parts are available on hire/rental from the publisher's Hire Library or appropriate agent.

Texts

I

I look up to the sky and its stars,

And down to the earth and the things that creep there.

And I consider in my heart how their creation

Was planned with wisdom in every detail.

See the heavens above like a tent,

Constructed with loops and with hooks,

And the moon with its stars, like a shepherdess

Driving her sheep to pasture;

The moon itself among the clouds,

Like a ship sailing under its banners;

The clouds like a girl in her garden

Moving, and watering the myrtle-trees;

The dew-mist—a woman shaking

Drops from her hair on the ground.

The inhabitants turn, like animals, to rest,

(Their palaces like their stables);

And all fleeing from the fear of death,

Like a dove pursued by the falcon.

And these are compared at the end to a plate

Which is smashed into innumerable shards.

Samuel ha-Nagid (993–1055/6), trans. David Goldstein

Text by Samuel ha-Nagid, translated by David Goldstein © Liverpool University Press.
Reproduced with permission of the Licensor through PLSclear.

II

I always loved this solitary hill,
This hedge as well, which takes so large a share
Of the far-flung horizon from my view;
But seated here, in contemplation lost,
My thought discovers vaster space beyond,
Supernal silence and unfathomed peace;
Almost I am afraid; then, since I hear
The murmur of the wind among the leaves,
I match that infinite calm unto this sound
And with my mind embrace eternity,
The vivid, speaking present and dead past;
In such immensity my spirit drowns,
And sweet to me is shipwreck in this sea.

Giacomo Leopardi (1798–1837), trans. Lorna de' Lucchi

III

Blazing, unmoving sun
over the isle of death,
the white stone house of Time.

They say it's where
eternal treasure dwells,
and if they say it,
it must be true.

On the table is a jug,
next to it a glass.

Whoever drinks from it forgets
their name and
loses their shape,

transforms into a grain of sand on the ground
on the blinding beach of the isle of death.

Doris Kareva (b. 1958), trans. Tiina Aleman

Text by Doris Kareva, translated by Tiina Aleman © Doris Kareva. Used by permission.

IV

O sun of real peace! O hastening light!

O free and extatic! O what I here, preparing, warble for!

O the sun of the world will ascend, dazzling, and take his height—

    and you too, O my Ideal, will surely ascend!

O so amazing and broad—up there resplendent, darting and burning!

O vision prophetic, stagger'd with weight of light! with pouring glories!

O lips of my soul, already becoming powerless!

O ample and grand Presidentiads! Now the war, the war is over!

New history! new heroes! I project you!

Visions of poets! only you really last! sweep on! sweep on!

O heights too swift and dizzy yet!

O purged and luminous! you threaten me more than I can stand!

(I must not venture—the ground under my feet menaces me—

    it will not support me:

O future too immense,)— O present, I return, while yet I may, to you.

Walt Whitman (1819–92)

This is the summit of contemplation, and

    no art can touch it

blue, so blue, the far-out archipelago

    and the sea shimmering, shimmering

no art can touch it, the mind can only

    try to become attuned to it

to become quiet, and space itself out, to

    become open and still, unworldcd

knowing itself in the diamond country, in

    the ultimate unlettered light.

Kenneth White (b. 1936)

'A high blue day on Scalpay' by Kenneth White © Kenneth White. Used by permission.

Splendor paternae gloriae,	*O splendour of the father's light,*
De luce lucem proferens,	*Bringing light out of light,*
Lux lucis et fons luminis,	*Light of light and source of light,*
Diem dies illuminans.	*Day lightening day.*
St Ambrose (c.340–397)	Translation by Henry Howard

V

Light the first light of evening, as in a room
In which we rest and, for small reason, think
The world imagined is the ultimate good.

This is, therefore, the intensest rendezvous.
It is in that thought that we collect ourselves,
Out of all the indifferences, into one thing:

Within a single thing, a single shawl
Wrapped tightly round us, since we are poor, a warmth,
A light, a power, the miraculous influence.

Here, now, we forget each other and ourselves.
We feel the obscurity of an order, a whole,
A knowledge, that which arranged the rendezvous.

Within its vital boundary, in the mind.
We say God and the imagination are one…
How high that highest candle lights the dark.

Out of this same light, out of the central mind,
We make a dwelling in the evening air,
In which being there together is enough.

Wallace Stevens (1879–1955)

'Final Soliloquy of the Interior Paramour' from *The Collected Poems Of Wallace Stevens* by Wallace Stevens © 1954 by Wallace Stevens and copyright renewed 1982 by Holly Stevens. Used by permission of Alfred A. Knopf, an imprint of the Knopf Doubleday Publishing Group, a division of Penguin Random House LLC. All rights reserved.

Commissioned by the Three Choirs Festival, UK, and the Elgin Master Chorale, USA.
In memory of my parents Giovanna Laurea Jackson (1931–2013) and Harry Francis Jackson (1930–2016)

THE WORLD IMAGINED

I

GABRIEL JACKSON

Samuel ha-Nagid (993–1055/6),
trans. David Goldstein

Music © Oxford University Press 2021. Text by Samuel ha-Nagid, translated by David Goldstein © Liverpool University Press.
Reproduced with permission of the Licensor through PLSclear.

Printed in Great Britain

OXFORD UNIVERSITY PRESS, MUSIC DEPARTMENT, GREAT CLARENDON STREET, OXFORD OX2 6DP
The Moral Rights of the Composer have been asserted. Photocopying this copyright material is ILLEGAL.

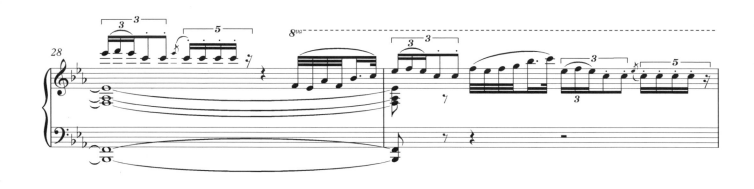

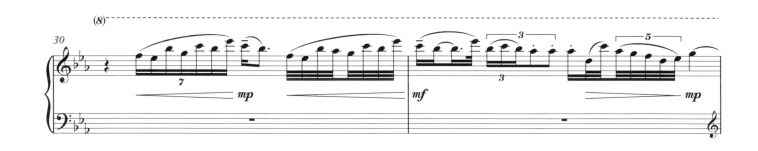

SOPRANOS *p*

I look____ up to the sky and its stars,____

ALTOS *p*

I look____ up____ to the sky and stars,____

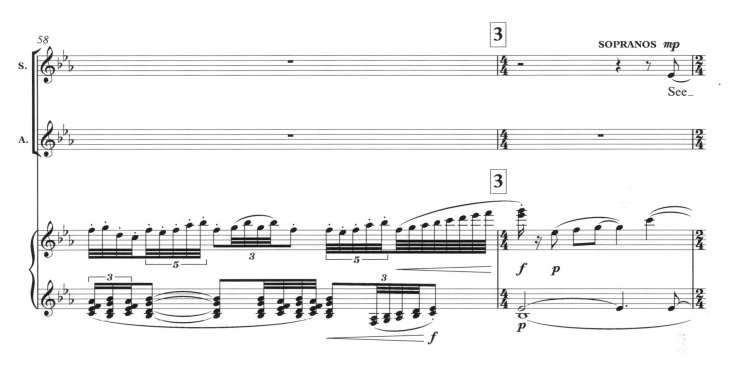

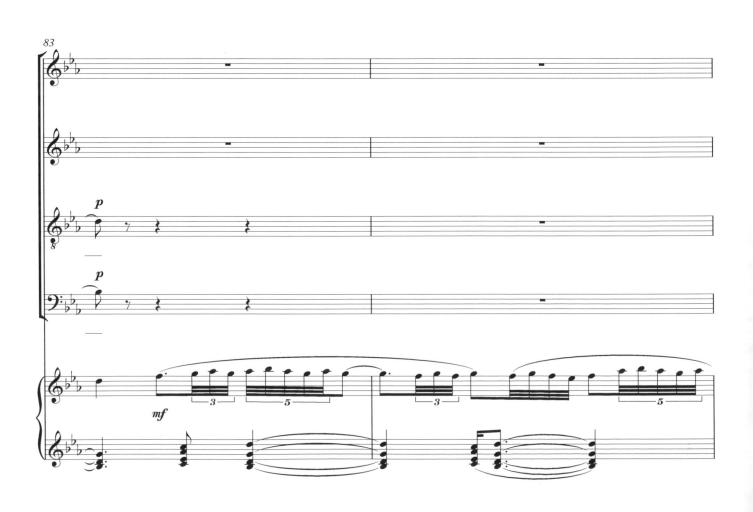

a - ni-mals, to rest,

a - ni-mals, to rest,

a - ni-mals, to rest,

a - ni-mals, to rest,

(Their pa - la - ces like their sta - bles);

(Their pa - la - ces like their sta - bles);

(Their pa - la - ces like their sta - bles);

(Their pa - la - ces like their sta - bles);

16

And

II

Giacomo Leopardi (1798–1837), trans. Lorna de' Lucchi

© Oxford University Press 2021. Photocopying this copyright material is ILLEGAL.

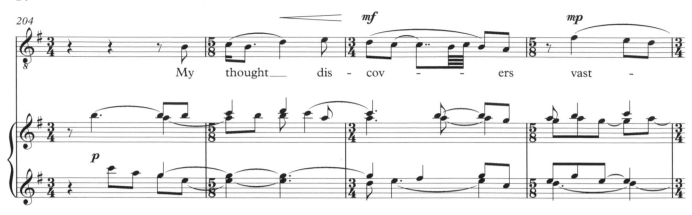

and un-fath - omed peace;

and un - fath-omed peace;

and un - fath-omed peace;

and un - fath-omed peace;

and un - fath-omed peace;

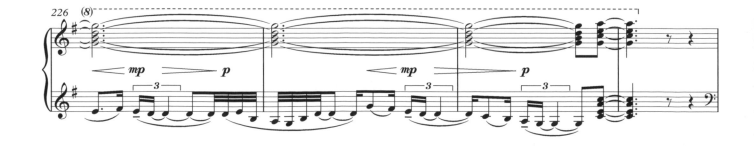

since I hear The mur - mur of the wind,

leaves,

leaves,

leaves,

leaves,

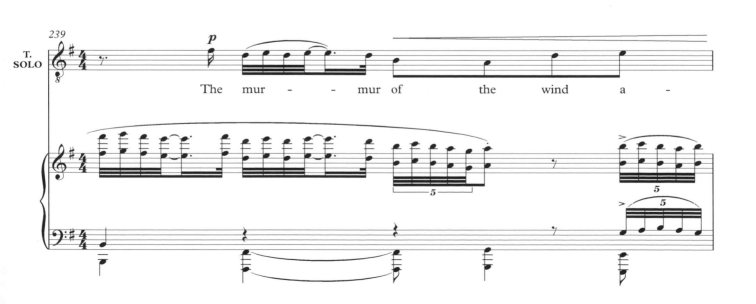

The mur - - mur of the wind a -

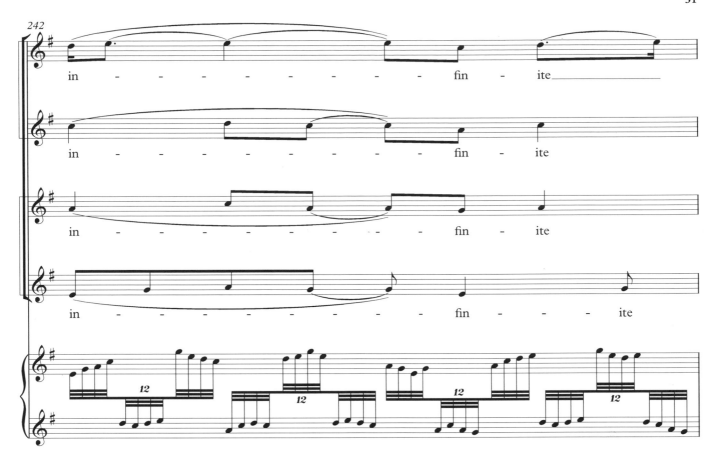

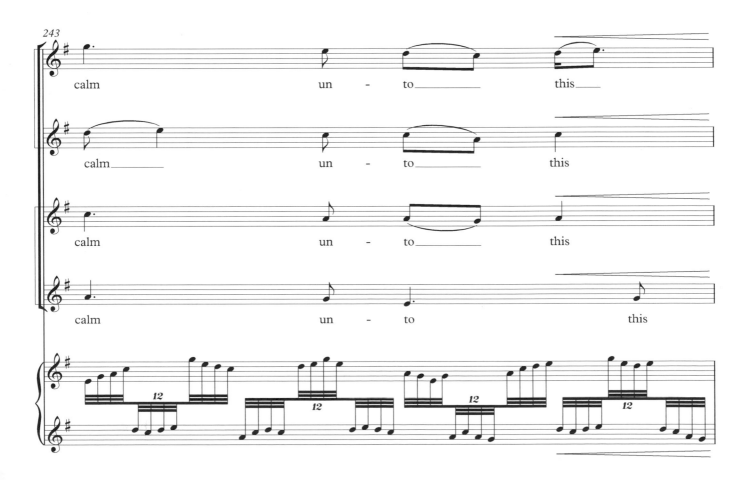

and dead past; In____ such im - men -

- - - - - - - si - ty my__ spi - - rit drowns,
-men - - - - - si - ty my__ spi - - rit drowns,__
-men - - - si - ty my____ spi - - rit drowns,
-men - - - si - ty my____ spi - - rit drowns,

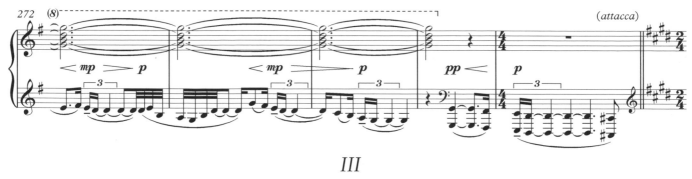

III

Doris Kareva (b. 1958), trans. Tiina Aleman

Music © Oxford University Press 2021. Text by Doris Kareva, translated by Tiina Aleman © Doris Kareva. Used by permission.

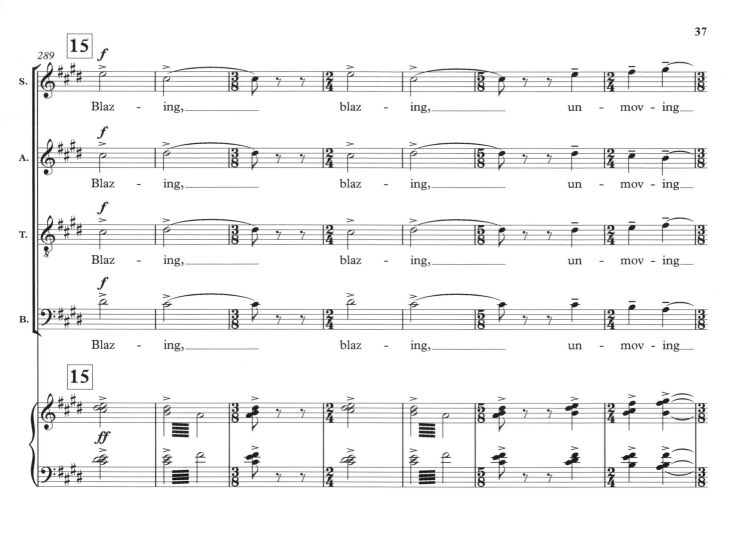

Blaz - ing,_____ blaz - ing,_____ un - mov - ing__

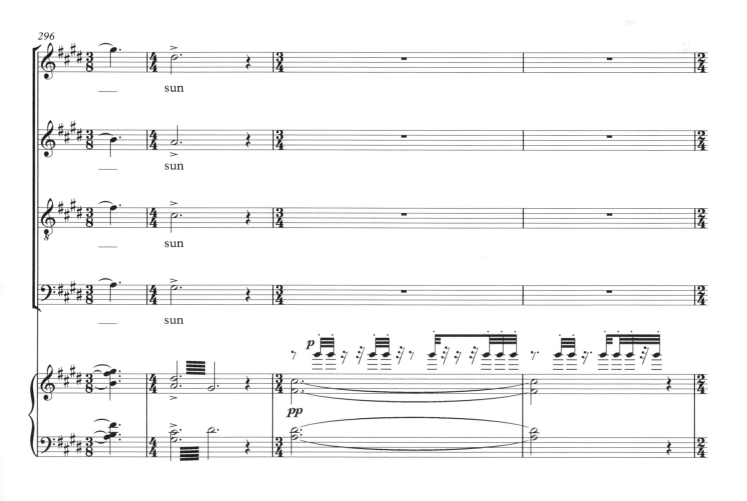

_____ sun

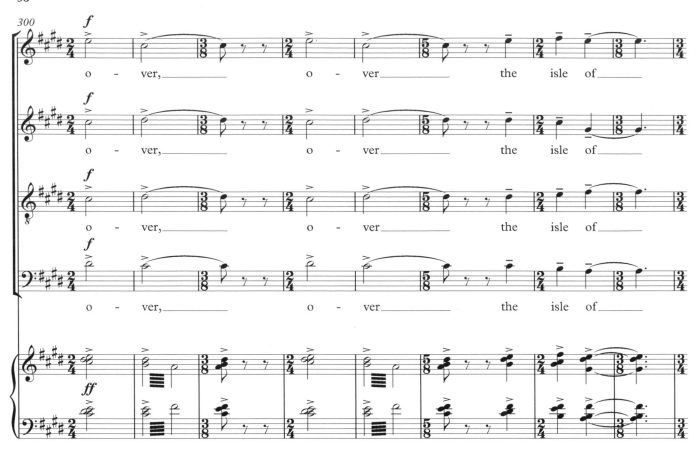

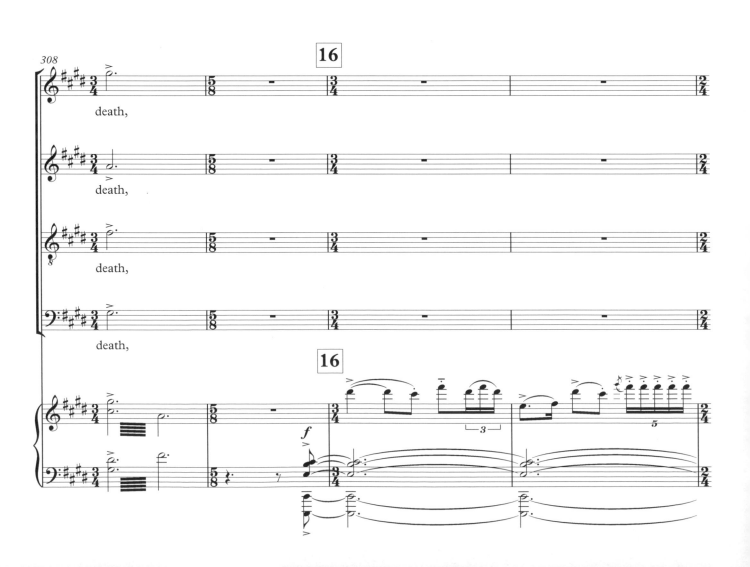

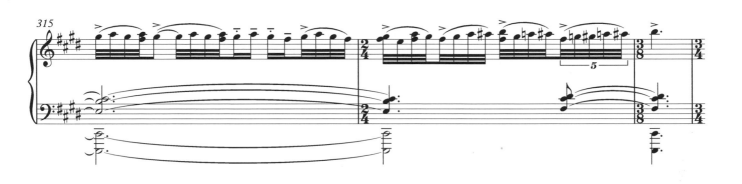

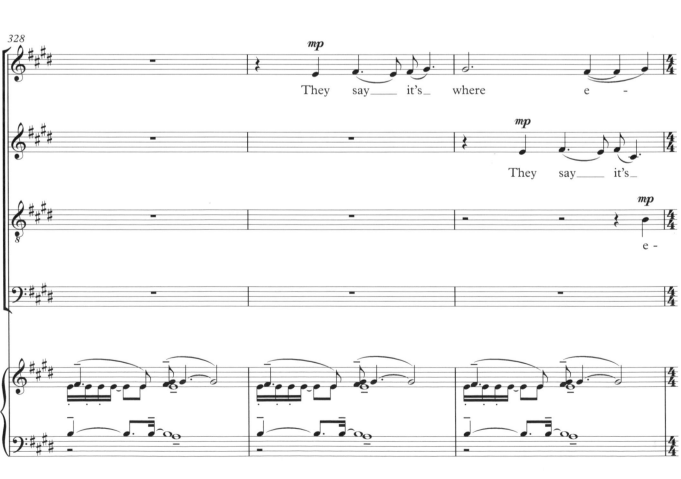

They say___ it's___ where e -

They say___ it's___

e -

SOPRANOS

On the ta - ble is a jug,

-ing_____ beach on the isle of_____ death,

-ing_____ beach on the isle of_____ death,

-ing_____ beach on the isle of_____ death,

-ing_____ beach on the isle of_____ death,

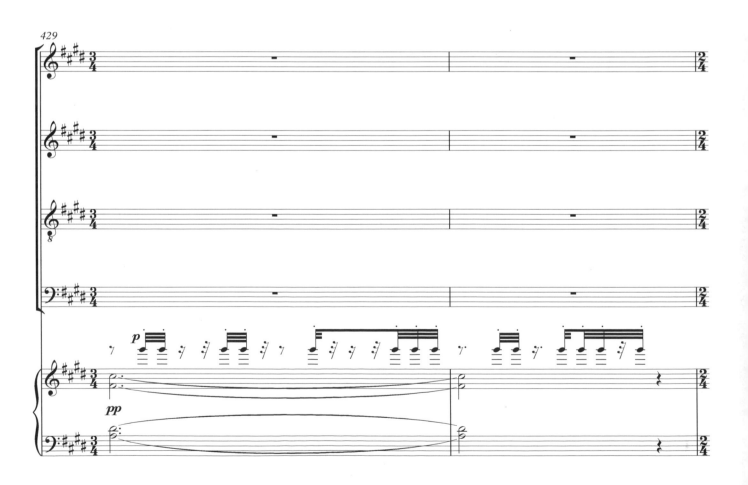

blind - ing____ beach, the blind - ing____ beach

blind - ing____ beach, the blind - ing____ beach

blind - ing____ beach, the blind - ing____ beach

blind - ing____ beach, the blind - ing____ beach

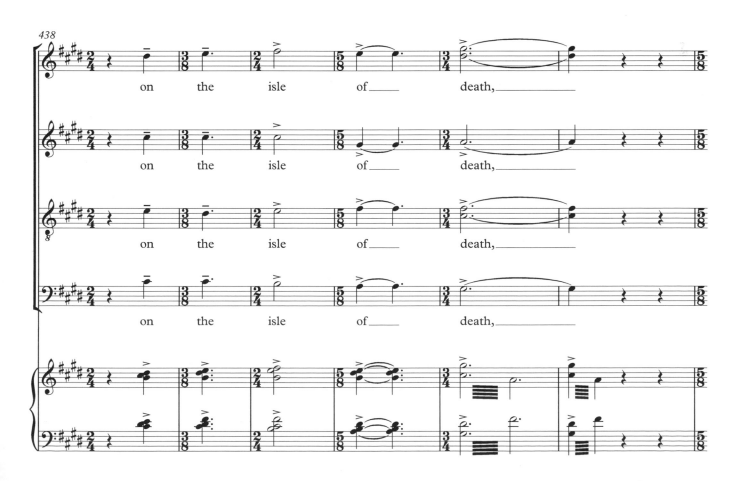

on the isle of ____ death,____

on the isle of ____ death,____

on the isle of ____ death,____

on the isle of ____ death,____

on the isle of death.

on the isle of death.

on the isle of death.

on the isle of death.

(attacca)

IV

Walt Whitman (1819–92)
Kenneth White (b. 1936)
St Ambrose (*c.*340–397)

Music © Oxford University Press 2021. 'A high blue day on Scalpay' by Kenneth White © Kenneth White. Used by permission.

O free_____ and ex - ta - - tic!

O free_____ and ex - ta - - tic!

O free_____ and ex - ta - - tic!

O free_____ and ex - ta - - tic!

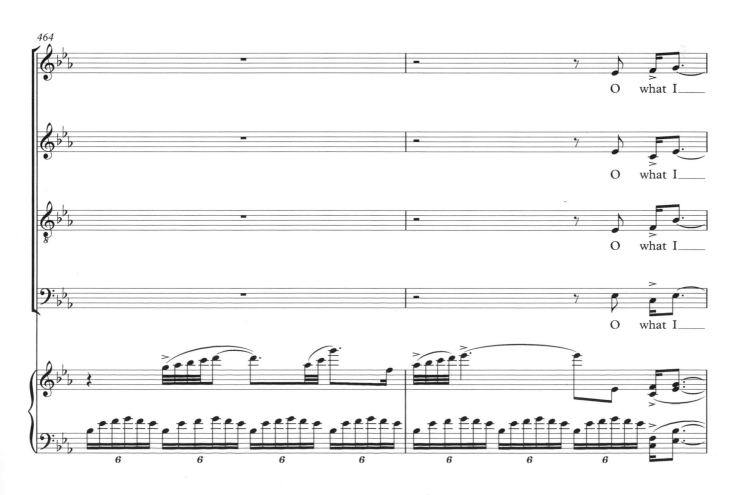

O what I____

O what I____

O what I____

O what I____

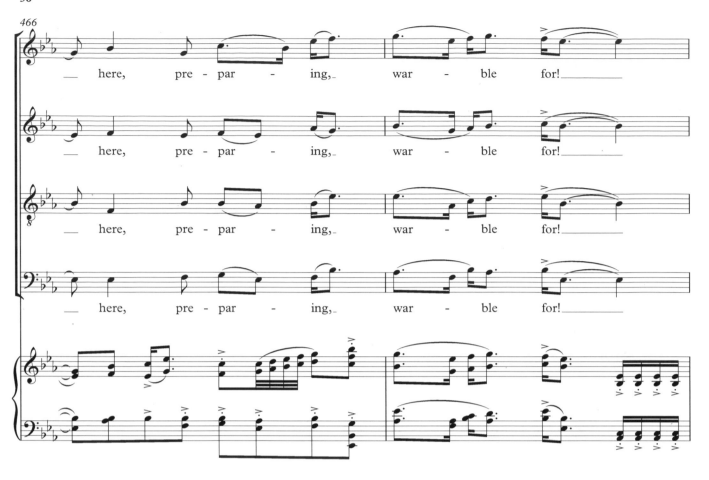

here, pre-par - ing,_ war - ble for!_

O_ the_ sun of the world_ will_ as-cend, daz - zling,_

and you too,___ O my I - deal,

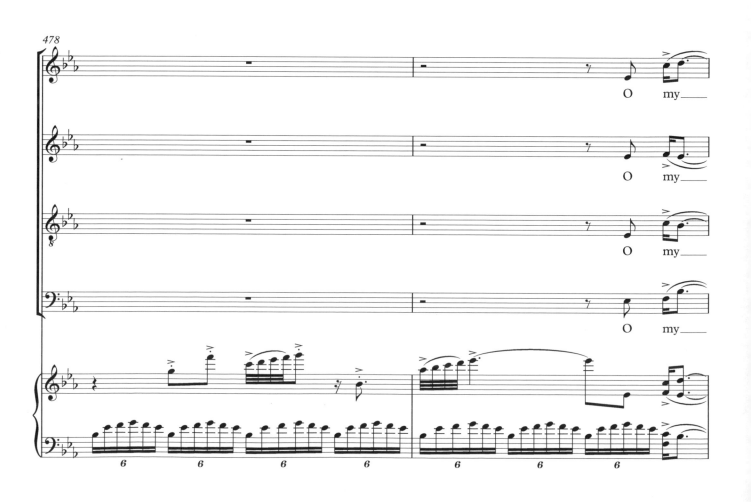

O my___

re - splen - - - - dent,___ dart-ing and burn - ing!_

re - splen - - - - dent,___ dart-ing and burn - ing!_

re - splen - - - - dent,___ dart-ing and burn - ing!_

re - splen - - - - dent,___ dart-ing and burn - ing!_

O vi - - - - sion___ pro - phet - ic,_

O vi - - - - sion___ pro - phet - ic,_

O vi - - - - sion___ pro - phet - ic,_

O vi - - - - sion___ pro - phet - ic,_

stag-ger'd_____ with weight_____ of light!_____

stag-ger'd_____ with weight_____ of light!_____

stag-ger'd_____ with weight_____ of light!_____

stag-ger'd_____ with weight_____ of light!_____

with pour - ing glo - ries!_____ O lips_____

with pour - ing glo - ries!_____ O lips_____

with pour - ing glo - ries!_____ O lips_____

with pour - ing glo - ries!_____ O lips_____

you threat-en me more than I can stand!____

you threat-en me more than I can stand!____

you threat-en me more than I can stand!____

you threat-en me more than I can stand!____

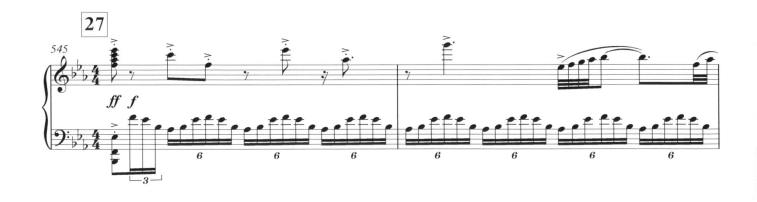

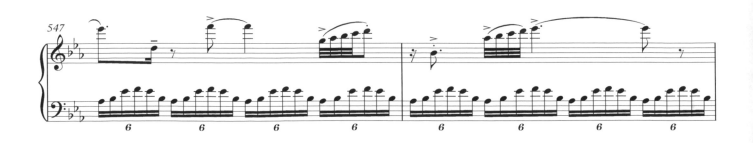

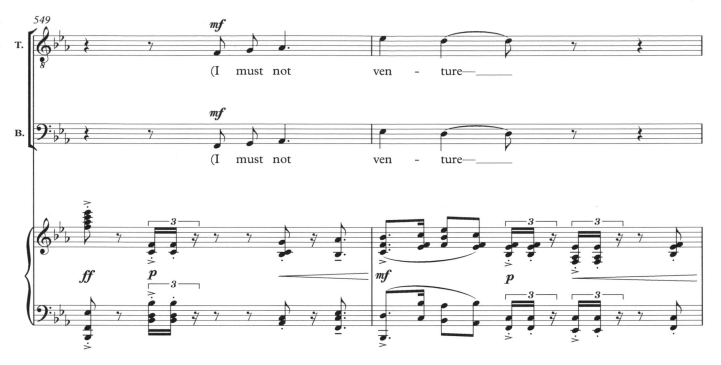

(I must not ven - ture——

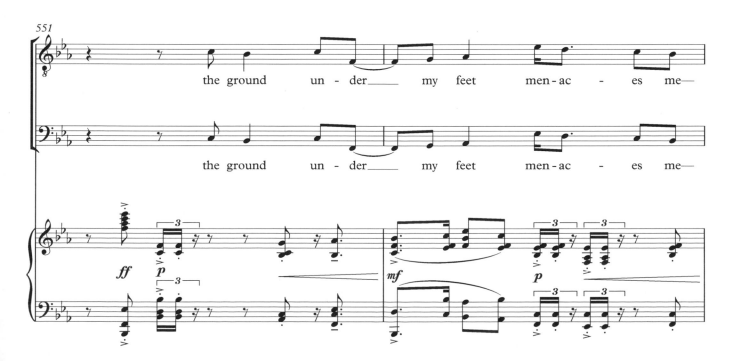

the ground un - der—— my feet men - ac - es me—

splen - - dor pa - ter - nae_____

glo - - - - ri - ae,

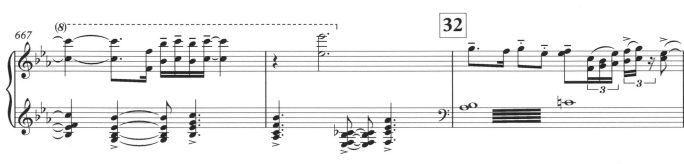

33

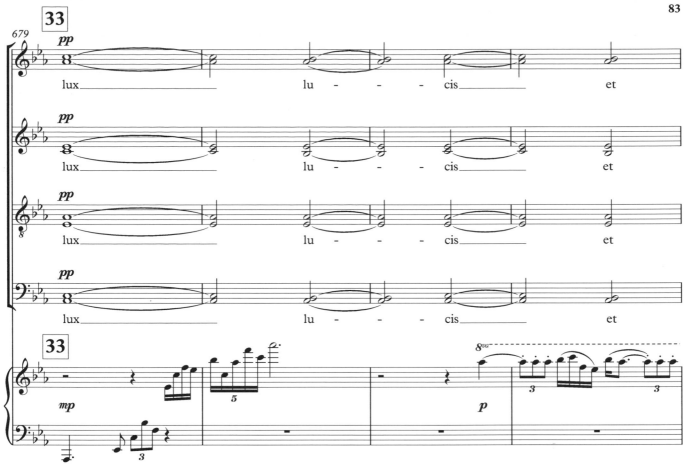

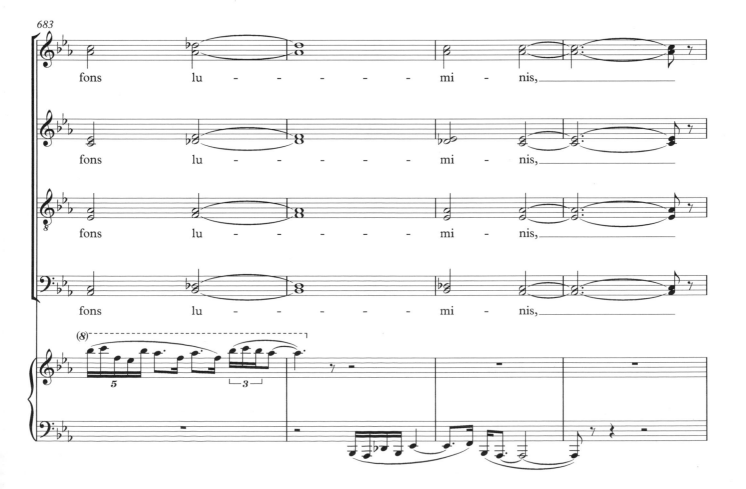

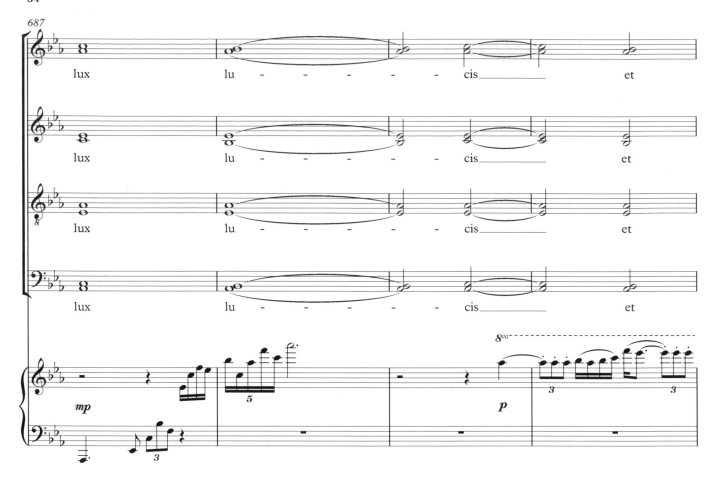

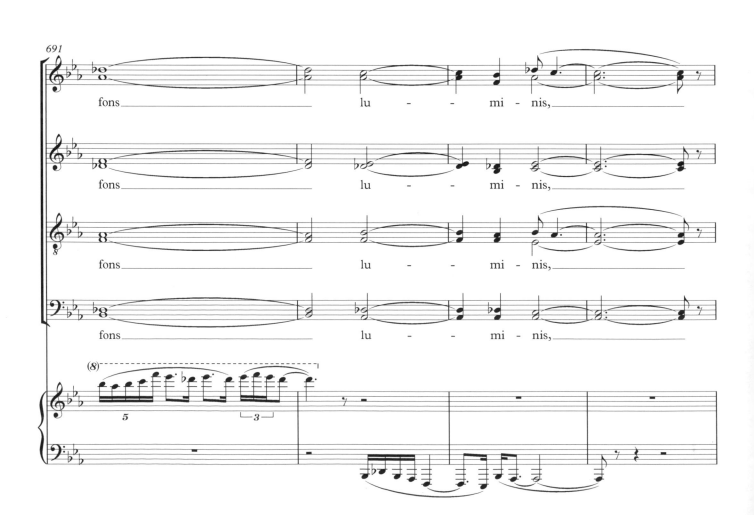

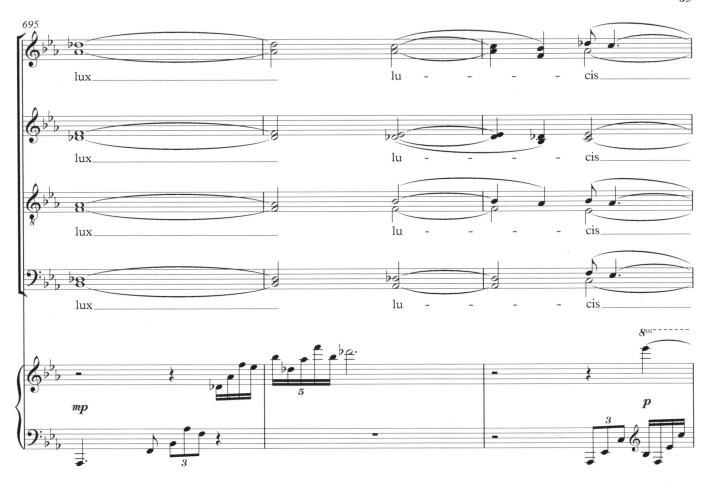

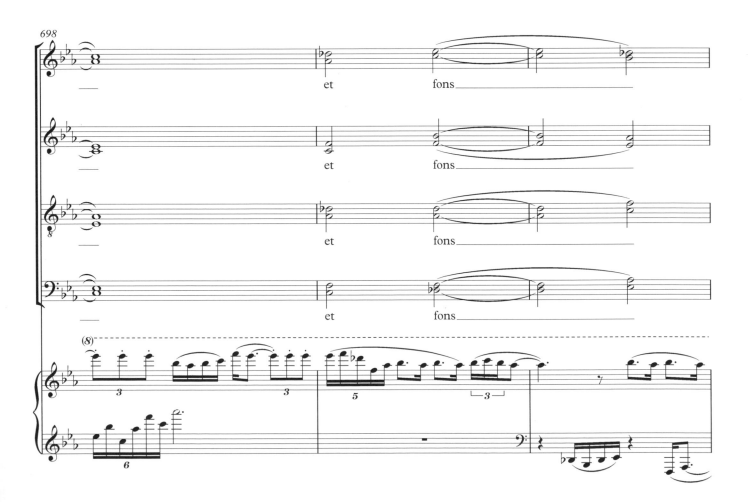

V

Wallace Stevens (1879–1955)

Music © Oxford University Press 2021. 'Final Soliloquy of the Interior Paramour' from *The Collected Poems Of Wallace Stevens* by Wallace Stevens © 1954 by Wallace Stevens and copyright renewed 1982 by Holly Stevens. Used by permission of Alfred A. Knopf, an imprint of the Knopf Doubleday Publishing Group, a division of Penguin Random House LLC. All rights reserved.

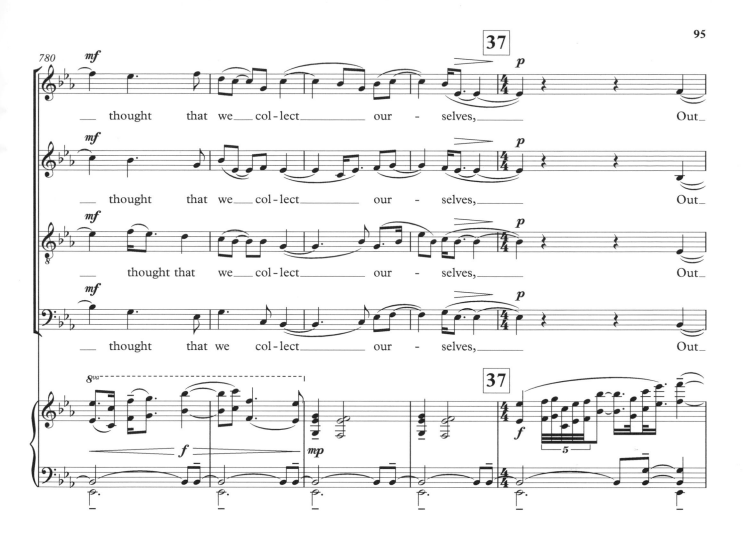

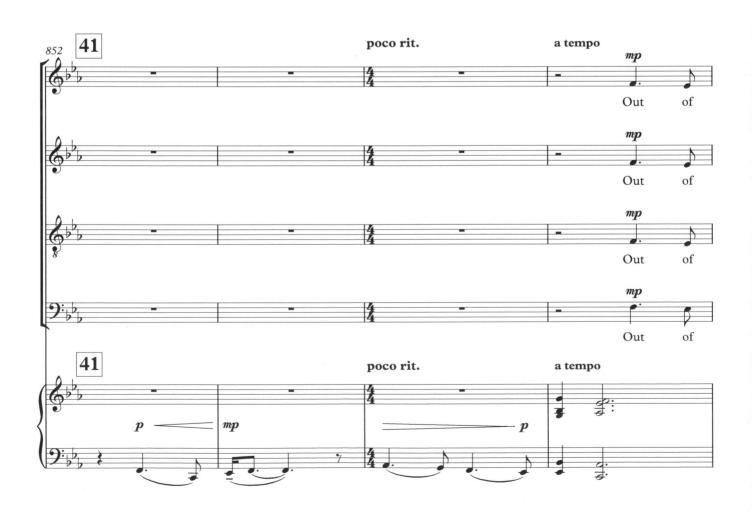

Brockley, June 2019–February 2020